Wordclay
1663 Liberty Drive, Suite 200
Bloomington, IN 47403
www.wordclay.com

First published by Wordclay on 10/19/2009.
ISBN: 978-1-6048-1656-3 (sc)

Printed in the United States of America.

This book is printed on acid-free paper.

God, Are You Kidding Me?

ೞ৪৫

Hearing from God in the echoes of His laughter...

By

Wendell C. Douglas

wordclay

Dedication

This book is dedicated to God, my friends, some related, some not, and all the students, teachers, and church folks whose paths I've crossed.

Most of all, to my wife and family, without whose delightful insanity and mine, this wonderful life would not have been possible.

Wendell C Douglas

Acknowledgements

I will always be indebted to the many church folks and families who have enriched my life with theirs. To those students and fellow teachers at Morgan City High School who endured my first professional years and who taught me so much about teaching, I say thanks! So many stories stemming from those early days decorate my thoughts daily.

I am particularly thankful for our children and their sense of humor, fierce family pride, and peculiar abilities to find humor in the oddest places and circumstances! I appreciate the time they spend laughing at me when I find myself in bizarre situations. They have allowed me to share our stories; they laugh at themselves, and rarely miss an opportunity make fun of each other. Through some very tough times, those are the gifts that defined and sustained us.

Finally, I must thank my wife, Melba, for having a heart of gold, for being a good sport, and for hanging in there through awful times.

W.C.D.

Table of Contents

INTRODUCTION

I used to believe that when God had something to say to me personally, He'd carve it in a rock, do a Super Bowl commercial, plaster it on a billboard, or send me an email or text message; I'd still be waiting to hear from Him if that were the case.

Only recently, while engaging in some age-induced retrospective thinking, I've discovered that God has been communicating with me all along. No, He hasn't rented a billboard or TV commercial time. In fact, He hasn't been a great communicator by most *human* standards. What He had been saying all along had been telegraphed loudly...and clearly! He'd been talking to me *in the echoes of His laughter!*

CHAPTER 1: THE POOP SCOOP

Ↄ

When I was much younger, had more hair, and completely blinded by the sparkle of stars in my eyes, I rarely went to bed without thinking, almost aloud, that being a minister was just an incredible privilege. The thought of being called "Reverend" always sent chills down my spine and left arm. This breezy, fall day had begun as many others had with my wife leaving to go to work to teach mentally challenged children and I, feeling quite pastoral, spending my day thinking of things to do to validate my existence.

Lucky for me, on this particular evening there was to be a wonderful celebration service at the tiny, red brick Baptist mission church where I was pastor, some thirty miles away from our Thibodaux, Louisiana home. Mission department dignitaries, dressed in their finest "we're-here-to-visit-the-little-church-in-the-swamp" garb would be there; my mind was filled with the possibilities of praise for my mission ministry efforts and hope for a promotion out of the swamp church!

Propped on my elbows in the bed, I daydreamed for a while about who would be at the evening service... I swallowed my last sip of strong, New Orleans-blend Community coffee, and eventually stumbled toward the shower. It was then the phone rang and the course of the day took a twisted, incredible turn. On the other end of the line was a mother of six children, whose husband was in a hospital in the city, really sick with emphysema.

"Can you take me to Baton Rouge to see my husband?"

"Sure," I replied, without a moment's hesitation. "Just give me a little time to get to your house."

I showered quickly, put on my pastoral slacks and jacket, and headed out to change the world.

The thirty mile trip to the church community seemed to whiz by. Gospel songs on the radio went pinging through my brain, and occasionally I joined in, feeling quite spiritual. My arrival at their mobile home was heralded by their barking Chihuahua and the two youngest children, swinging on the door knob of the open front door.

"Get in Brother Wendell's car. We are going to see Daddy."

With a bounce and a leap, the backseat of our yellow, 1973 Plymouth Duster, nicknamed "Honey" by my wife, became the roost for the two little ones, T-Boo and Maryanne.

"We need to stop at the store. I need to get something," the mom instructed as we backed out of the driveway. The peculiar, distinctive odor of fresh onions pretty much gave away the "something" that needed to be purchased at the Seven-Eleven down the street. I sat in the car with the two little ones while she ran inside. Once back in the car, and as we pulled out of the store's parking lot, she slathered on some kind of white, rose-scented deodorant cream under each arm, creating yet another aromatic assault. This is the ministry, I thought. This is the ministry.

Before long, the trip to the hospital took on a life of its own. Each stop light, and there were many, elicited a cautionary warning from my three passengers, shouting in unison, "It's red!" or "It's green!"

This game was not cute in the city where every ten feet down a street or highway is celebrated by a stop light. My brain began to ache. The rosebud and onion soup smells had made me nauseous. I began to doubt this whole ministry thing...

About halfway back home, after an incredibly difficult day, I noticed that T-Boo, clad in faded blue short pants and bright red tee-shirt, had grown very quiet and had shifted to the far corner of the back seat.

Maryanne and her mom, however, were engaged in another challenging game of saying to each other, "You're one more!" answered by the other with, "Nah ah, *you're* one more."

It didn't take long to discover why T-Boo had moved over to the corner. It must have been a privacy thing as he proceeded to soil his pants. Five years old. Soiling of the pants is a significant event for a five-year-old. It's significant for those in the car, as well. As we finally arrived back at their house, they asked if we would pick them up for church.

"Sure, but T-Boo, be sure you take a bath," I encouraged.

A thirty-mile rush back home, a quick shower, and my wife and I were ready to head back to the church. Of course, we were the main transportation for many of our parishioners, so we started the community rounds, picking up kids for the special evening service. Imagine my alarm when I noticed T-Boo was wearing the same clothes! No bath. Oh, mercy. My suspicions were confirmed when he, along with several other kids, climbed into "Honey," layered and seat-belted two kids deep across the back seat. The odor of T-Boo's earlier problem was horrible. The other kids were gagging and trying to huff the outside air through fold-out back windows**.**

Winding around the swamp road curves and dodging junk in the road, we couldn't get to the church fast enough. As the kids bailed out of the car, I noticed that many "dignitaries" had arrived. Man, they were dressed up, expecting a wonderful evening service. Oh lord...I spotted the sponsoring pastor, shaking hands with the just-arrived head of the state missions department. The swarm of kids, clamoring out of the car and hustling to get away from T-Boo, burst through the closed cypress doors, blew past the visiting pastors, and down the aisle of the church.

Before they could be corralled, T-Boo's oldest sister, leading the pack, felt compelled to explain why they were running into the church, and announced loudly and clearly.... "T-Boo crapped in his pants!"

12

Well... before I could become part of the dignified service, I had to escort T-Boo, quite impacted by now, to the restroom to relieve him of his burden. With a wooden spatula and nearly a roll of toilet paper I got him back in shape. I gagged. A lot. The ministry. Got to love it.

Dear God,

Why is it that sometimes great expectations just somehow turn to poop?

Amen.

CHAPTER 2: PLEASE HURRY UP!

CᴓƷ

Children. Just the mention of the word conjures sweet images of blowing fragile bubbles into the wind, giggles and laughter, running into a full hug across a school yard at the end of a long day, Christmas mornings filled with wonder and excitement…wow.

Our precocious little princess came into our lives as a frightened, wide-eyed eighteen-month old, in the arms of our foster care social worker, but soon hit the ground running. Her mother and I beamed with pride as she finished her paramedic training, graduated from nursing school, and then law school. As aspiring attorneys were called forward across the stage to receive their hard-earned Loyola Law School diplomas, we beamed, and I started having flashbacks to her childhood…

Standing up in the back, cypress board pew of the little swamp church, our princess, three years old, had already made several noisy trips up and down the length of the pew, always just out of reach of her mother's frustrated attempts to grab her frilly coattail. The music part of the church service was finished, and I had begun a wonderfully inspiring sermon about something.

Our little lady was the embodiment of hyperactivity, a strong will, and a contentious spirit. Never content to just sit and *be*, she busied herself with everyone else's business, and voiced her opinion at will. No amount of coaxing, bribery, or threats seemed to cause a change in her antics.

Because I was a student of the "visualize and realize" philosophy (*what you see is what you get*) I sometimes tried to visualize what preaching in a very large auditorium would be like. I'd visualize TV cameras, lights, large viewing screens...oh yes! However, missing from my mental picture was an obnoxious little girl, prancing up and down the pew in her little noisy, black, patent-leather shoes. Shooting grimacing faces at her seemed to prod her on. In fact, she mimicked a frown I sent her way, and I almost lost it.

As a pastor, I was determined to model proper parenting for my parishioners. I managed a little grin that was supposed to say, "She's going to get it later."

Instead, one of the older ladies felt free to pipe up, "That's what's wrong...you laugh at 'em, and they don't respect you." It was on then.

"Excuse me a moment," I said to the congregation. "I need to speak to my daughter."

"Mommy, is he going to spank me?" a tiny voice yelled from the back of the church. My wife was red. Crimson red.

I stalked to the back pew, brushed past my wife, and whispered in my precious darling's ear, "If you don't settle down NOW, I'm going to take you out of here and you're going to get it!"

As soon as I turned my back, and with an appropriate, but temporary sad little face, she eased down against the back of the pew, jerking away from my wife's attempt to scoot her closer. I triumphantly strode back to the pulpit, confident that I had overcome, conquered, and changed my little lady's attitude forever. In a flash I remembered her nearly getting me arrested at the mall while she stuffed merchandise down into the side of her stroller (I still don't think the security people believed me). I recalled that from the back of a shopping cart she pulled the braided hair of a screaming little girl. I remembered her threatening to beat up her older brother with a hair dryer and squeezing the stuffing out of her

15

first kitten…what a delightful blessing. All taken care of, now. It was fixed. Daddy had spoken.

Picking up my three-inch thick, over-sized Bible, and taking a deep breath, I felt like the star of *"Father Knows Best,"* and triumphantly resumed my sermon. My next point was to be the hook, line, and sinker that brought everyone home to Jesus.

Just as I leaned into the pulpit, in the most pastoral, hushed tone I could create, a tiny voice from the back pew shouted at the top of her lungs, "Daddy, would you hurry up? I'm hungry!" She won. Game over.

Dear God,

Exactly, what does "suffer the little children" mean? How about "spare the rod?" Just thinking.

Amen

CHAPTER 3: ALL BY ITSELF

ॐ

God must have a sense of humor. That's the only logical explanation for calling me into the ministry and then into education. Either way, I was sentenced to learn something new everyday. I had just been appointed the assistant principal of a middle school, and nothing but joy filled every moment. My main tasks each day consisted of discipline, assigning detention, counseling angry parents, and trying to get a Commodore 64 computer to sort 350, five-field records in under an hour.

On this rather routine Thursday, the computer was winning yet another round of our ongoing battle of wits. I was interrupted by the swishing of stockings and clacking of teacher steps charging up the hall from the direction of the fourth grade classrooms. Almost in unison, the sounds of smaller feet, marching with purpose and business, accompanied the teacher's cadence.

"Hmmmm," I thought, "If that entourage is headed here, I need to look busy and put my game face on."

I know, simple thoughts, but real.

I had recently swallowed my pride and purchased a pair of gold-rimmed reading glasses which I came to enjoy. I wore them on the end of my nose so that when I had to yell at students, I could look really intense by peering over the top of the lenses. I loved the look. As the steps got closer, I quickly adjusted my glasses and braced for the onslaught. Around the corner and through my door burst the teacher with a skinny little gentleman in tow. Right behind her filed in four teary, visibly shaken young ladies, all with Kleenex in one hand and each other's hand in the other.

16

"Do you see this young man?" she asked.

"Do you know what he did?"

She gave him a disgusted glance that should have shamed him, but he never flinched. He was a curious little lad, sporting a baseball shirt and a pair of gray, jogging pants, hoisted nearly to his armpits. His huge, round, red glasses framed his face as he peered back at me. Nope, she hadn't budged him.

"What exactly did he do?" I asked, with curiosity about to kill me.

"Well, we'll tell you what he did." She lined up the young ladies, who by this time were heaving and squalling in a chorus, and asked each to step forward, one at a time, to tell their tales.

"I...saw...his...thing," the first one sobbed.

I immediately sent Lawrence to stand in the outer hall while the other girls testified. He quickly exited.

"I saw it, too!" the next one offered in a hoarse, serious whisper.

The next young lady, readying herself for her testimony, completely lost it. Loud wailing and racking sobs, followed by ceremonious eye dabbing, interrupted her many false starts.

"Take a deep breath," I urged. "It's ok."

Summoning all the courage she could, she dabbed one last time and stared me right in the eye.

"I saw it, too, and he *pointed* it at me."

For the life of me, I couldn't remember a single graduate class that taught the proper way to deal with fourth grade nastiness.

Not a single one. Guessing I was going to have to wing this one, I sent the ladies out and asked Lawrence to come back into my office.

Calling upon my most serious game face, over the glasses and all, I glared at Lawrence, hiked up breeches and all, and asked the ultimate question. "Did you show them your *thing*?"

Peering back through his big, oval, red-rimmed glasses, he answered, "Yes, sir."

"Did you *point* it at them?" And his answer to that question, to this day, still blows me away.

"No sir." he answered stoically. "It did it all by itself."

Dear God,

So, when things take on a life of their own, are you still in charge?

Amen.

CHAPTER 4: THE DIRTY DOZEN

ॐ

There truly are occupational hazards in being a minister. People sometimes just seem compelled to do things for you.

Early in our little swamp church ministry, I awoke one morning with the bright idea that we could be more effective if we actually lived in the community where the church was located.

My poor wife, the sheltered, only child of elderly parents, and who would agree to anything, said, "Sure, why not?"

So, we hitched up our mobile home, where my wife and I, along with our two mutts, had lived since our wedding, and headed to the swamp. Alligators, snakes, spiders, and some very interesting neighbors welcomed us to our new neighborhood.

Our new neighbors, loud, raucous and interesting, were very gracious and proud of their place. They had made a home from a small, beat-up travel trailer, with a lean-to attached to the side. I never could quite figure out how they survived, but they seemed to always have gas and grocery money. They became our "swamp life" mentors, offering every kind of advice imaginable about living in an area where spring flooding often made the roads impassable. At night, the loudest cacophony imaginable of croaking, thumping, and screeching of swamp life kept us awake. Mosquitoes the size of Rhode Island were everywhere. Yep, we were living large. What a brilliant idea, moving to the swamp and all.

One day, sensing our despair, I suppose, our neighbors did a neighborly thing. I'll never forget it. Earlier in the afternoon, after shaving her husband's back in the front yard, she poured kerosene over the fresh-shaved area, causing him to yell and cuss very loudly. I wince, still, just thinking about it.

"How the hell you want me to kill all the nits if I don't put the kerosene?" she yelled at him.

He didn't answer. He couldn't hear her over his own painful moans. She must have seen me staring in awe at the spectacle. She threw up her hands and waved at me, telling me she had a surprise for us later.

A big barrel sat next to their lean-to, catching rain water as it drained off the roof. He pumped water from it occasionally with a hand pump attached to the side.

"Come look what I got in here," he hollered at me, pointing to the barrel.

I strolled over, expecting to see a barrel full of rainwater....but shocked at what I saw. About ten of the biggest, greenish swamp turtles I had ever seen were clamoring near the top of the barrel, half floating and half swimming in the barrel of water.

"I'm going to kill a couple of 'em later and the ole lady's going to make some turtle soup."

So that was the surprise. I could handle turtle soup, but I knew my wife couldn't.

"I bet that'll be good," I offered, not wanting to sound very interested...and hoping to avoid an invitation

The afternoon wore on, and dark was closing in. A kick on our door announced the neighbor's arrival, with both hands holding a lime green, plastic plate, upon which sat one of the most beautiful milk-chocolate covered cakes I'd ever seen.

"I brought y'all a cake. It's yellow on the inside, but chocolate icing."

Thanking her profusely, I accepted the cake and gave her a hug. It wasn't long before we were digging into the cake...moist and delicious, for sure! My wife transferred the rest of the cake to one of our own dishes so that we could return the neighbor's plate the next day.

Strolling back over to their place, the empty plate in hand, I broke into compliments and yummy talk, even before she stepped out of their trailer.

"That cake was delicious! My wife wanted to know...how did you get the cake so yellow and moist?"

"That cake better be yellow and moist....I cut nearly a dozen eggs out those two turtles we ate and put 'em in the cake mix."

Dear God,

I hate it when things aren't what they appear to be!

Amen.

CHAPTER 5: THE WEDDING

ᙉ

Few celebrations in life can even begin to embrace the solemn loveliness of a wedding. The carefully selected flowers, the nervous brides, the fussy mothers and tuxedoed gentlemen all come together with soft music and supportive guests to make the very special occasion truly worshipful and special. At the little church in the swamp, one such occasion just didn't rise to that level of acclaim. Oh, the intent was truly there, but here's how it happened that hot, humid Saturday in August.

I had suspected the building was a hurry-up job, built by a local contractor, out of spare parts. The air conditioner's air return was just behind the pulpit. Loud, whistling breezes swept by—when it worked—muffling the preacher and causing the congregation to lean forward, straining to hear. The AC didn't cool very well, and on this Saturday, with a wedding slated for two o'clock, I decided it would be expedient to turn the AC on early, just to get the building comfortable for the service. I jetted over to the church, flipped on the switch, and headed back home…satisfied that the celebration would come off without a hitch.

I always try to arrive early for special occasions, just in case last minute changes happen. Today, however, was an exception. For some reason, time had slipped away from me, and I arrived at church just five minutes before the wedding was to begin. I wasn't really concerned, though, because I knew the building would be cool and comfortable. I knew everything would be fine because I had left a key with the wedding party, and they would be ready to roll on schedule!

Well, the nauseating, stomach-wrenching sight of the windows up, the curtains tied in knots, and the doors standing wide-open greeted me as I pulled into the gravel covered parking lot.

"What in the world?" I inquired with growing anxiety. "Is the AC working?

"Nope, it sure ain't," was the reply from the groom.

This was not good. Not a breeze was stirring, the humidity was near 100%, and the little church was full. However, being an undying optimist, I gingerly urged everyone to take their places so that we could get started. We lined up, the groomsmen in the back of the building and the bridesmaids in the front. Last minute instructions from me to them would have them follow me to their places as I strode to the podium.

As soon as I began my strut to the podium, the groom's mother shouted out, "Wait. Don't start yet. The music man ain't here yet."

The music man. Darn. In the dismay over the AC system, I had not noticed that there was no music playing. Even though the music man had not been present for practice, they had assured me he would be there for the wedding, playing appropriate music. We waited. We sweated, we fanned, and we waited.

Finally, after thirty minutes of waiting in the sweltering heat, having to make an executive decision, I declared the wedding must start. Everyone took their places…groomsmen to the back, bridesmaids in the front. The bridesmaids strode in, fanning, met by the groomsmen, now in Tee-shirts and very sweaty. They all took their places.

Just as the bride and her father entered the front doors of the church, everyone's attention was jerked to the windows by the screeching of tires and the slinging of loose gravel everywhere. Applause erupted, welcoming the music man.

"Wait up!" the groom's mother shouted from the front row.

"He's here. She can walk in to the music." Everyone applauded.

The music man unloaded an electric organ of dubious quality from the back end of a dusty white, hatch-back Mazda. Dragging the dangling black cord behind him, he stumbled slightly toward the side door, and strode confidently across the auditorium, overly excusing himself as he bumped through the wedding party and several guests. I watched in utter amazement as I completely lost control of the situation. I glanced at the parents, and they had the look of a "job well done" on their faces as the music man prepared to play.

I glanced at the bridesmaids, hair hanging wet from sweat, as they gazed with envy at the patient bride, still at the front door, waiting to enter whenever the music man would begin to play. With a start, I noticed that the music man had tough, whiskey-smelling breath, lit a cigarette, and was about to play. In one fell swoop, I stepped forward, took the cigarette from his lips, and nodded a "let's begin" signal to him.

The bride, veil plastered to her face from sweat, and her father, suit coat over his wringing wet arm, stood poised for those first steps. It was at that moment the loud, unmistakable first notes began to fill the air. The song? Hank Williams' 1949 hit, "*I'm So Lonesome I Could Cry.*"

The wedding party and guests, loving the music, dabbed tears and sweat, and the knot was tied.

Dear God,

Are you suggesting that I be flexible?

Amen.

Chapter 6: The Piano Player

❦

The church piano was a cherry wood, upright, beautifully polished gift from *someone* to the little swamp church. No one could play it, but it looked so nice! Desperate for music of some kind, I had bought a little cheap, Western Auto guitar, taught myself a few chords, and wrote a few choruses that I could play…with the four chords I had learned! We had music…kind of.

Being the spiritual folks we were, we prayed every Sunday for God to send a piano player so that we could sing the hymns from the new hymnals, also given by some anonymous donor. I encouraged the congregation to "believe and receive." They believed. They believed.

One particular Sunday, an old blue Chevrolet Impala, grumbling muffler, smoke, and all, rolled into the parking lot, bearing the answer to our prayer. A portly lady, brown stringy hair wound into a tight top knot, stepped out with a tow-headed toddler tagging behind. She was Ms Camille. She was to be "our answered prayer."

Camille introduced herself to everyone as a God-led, recent arrival to the swamp from Florida and parts beyond. She, along with her husband and child, had rented a camp down the road and wished to make their life there. What an inspiring story. In fact, we were so proud of a new addition to the church family that my wife and I accepted her invitation to lunch--turkey and dressing--after church that very day!

Upon entering the little church, she spotted the polished, untouched piano sitting silent at the front of the church.

"Who plays the piano?" she whispered to one of our mission volunteer ladies.

"Do you play?" the volunteer asked excitedly.

"I sure do." Camille answered confidently, as she shed her Bible, toddler, and shoes, and darted toward the piano.

"Brother Wendell, our prayers have been answered! We have a piano player!"

"God is *so* good!" I exclaimed with awe-inspiring intonation.

"Everyone pick up a hymnal and turn to page 325, *"What A Friend We Have in Jesus."* Let's stand as we sing!"

I had been a music director in my earlier days, so the "rise, ready, sing" motions of a hymn-director's hands and arms took over my body. Of course, with the down-stroke of my hand, ready-to play Camille would commence the first notes of the old, familiar hymn.

Ready, set, and with the down swing of my hand, the most gosh-awful noise I had ever heard came banging from the piano. Camille was slapping the keys like she was swatting flies, without a single recognizable note coming from that piano. She had a far-away look on her face, as though she was channeling a concert pianist, live from Carnegie Hall.

The children burst out in uncontrollable laughter. The look of shock and disbelief left adult mouths gaping open. I had long since stopped singing and was staring at Camille, still banging away on the piano, nearing the end of the second verse. I quickly stepped to the piano and flagged her down.

In a stroke of genius, I had everyone bow their heads, and directed everyone into "a spirit of prayer." It was during this prayer that "God led me" to start preaching. Whew. The relief, however, was short-lived. The slow dawning of remembering that we had accepted a lunch invitation began to creep in. My wife, who had long-since gone pale, had the same lunch-time realization as I.

"What are we going to do?" she mouthed to me as I prayed.

I mouthed back, "We *have* to go." Oh mercy.

I figured at least we'd get to meet her husband, and invite him to church.

The black candle in the window should have tipped us off. She introduced him as a "devil worshiper" and that he didn't plan to have lunch with us.

We sat at the counter, waving off flies, wondering when lunch would be ready, since there was no evidence of turkey or dressing or anything. As Camille chattered and her toddler played, she busied herself by taking out a pot, a loaf of bread, and two turkey legs. We watched in silence as she filled the boiler with water, and put in on the stove's right front burner. Into the now-boiling water, she placed the two turkey legs and several slices of bread. She seasoned it with salt and pepper.

"Lunch should be ready in about five minutes," she announced.

A quick thinker,, I came up with some lame reason, and we dodged that bullet. Hustling out the door, my wife began to breathe again. At the kitchen window, from behind the pentagram and the flickering candle, her husband grinned as we pulled away. My wife sat shaking. I was very quiet…and a brand new student of life lessons.

Dear God,

I should be careful what I pray for. Is that it?

Amen.

CHAPTER 7: TIMING *Is* EVERYTHING

ɷ

Some emotion-based, 1980's educational theory came along and completely ruined my cut and dried approach to school administration. As a disciplinarian, my approach was relatively simple…follow the handbook. There are actions, which cause reactions. There are causes, which produce an effect. There are behaviors, which will get you into detention, suspension, or expulsion. Simple enough. Well, somewhere between being the necessary SOB and the requisite hand-holder and counselor, I was exposed to the "school of thought" that says schools should be kinder, gentler places. I decided to try this theory.

I had been appointed to the principal's position of an elementary school…a great place by anyone's standards. Elementary school teachers are delightfully energized, over-worked, and generally patient folks who genuinely care about kids. Trying out this new-to-me approach to develop a warm, welcoming school climate, would take place in a wonderful environment safe for new approaches. The school climate was already warm and friendly!

"I'll model what they do naturally!" I thought to myself. "I can do this."

My test case was a youngster who had reportedly witnessed his mom being beaten. He needed a warm, friendly comfort zone and the school was the natural place for him to emotionally recover. I easily hugged him and walked him to class. His teacher hugged him, and he rejoined his classmates, who were also warm and friendly.

"I like this," I whispered to myself. "Feels good."

Before I knew it, the makeover was complete. I was a hugger, a back patter, and a completely "interested-appearing" participant in the most trivial of conversations. From behind my principal's desk, the view of the school was nearly panoramic. I peered through rose-colored windows at the Mecca-like campus of Warm and Friendly. Life was good.

On this particular day, as I did the well-practiced principal stroll down the hallway, I could hear the sobs of a child, obviously upset about something. Not seeing anyone else in the hallway, I picked up my pace and walked toward the little lady, now standing, leaning against the hallway wall.

"What's wrong?" I asked as I squatted down to be eye-level with her. No answer, just tears and soft crying.

She held a crumbled hall pass in one hand, and I reached to hold her other hand to walk her to the office. She glanced warily at me, quickly scratched her head, and reached for my hand. Feeling very fulfilled, she and I proceeded down the hallway to the school office.

"Did you send for her?" I inquired of the school secretary.

She nodded an emphatic "yes" as she continued her conversation on the phone. She motioned with her free hand for the little girl to be seated. The little lady didn't move. She steadfastly stood there, still crying, and becoming even more upset.

Now what was a warm and friendly convert to do? I thought of my own daughter, my sons, and wondered what I'd like for someone to do if they were upset. That was it. My fatherly instincts kicked in. I reached to hug the little girl who quickly hugged me back...and held on.

"Ahem!" the secretary tapped loudly on her desk to get my attention as the little girl continued her hug.

29

"I know she can't be that hard-nosed," I thought. "If any kid ever needed a hug, this was it."

The secretary wagged her head from side to side, obviously disapproving of my attempts to comfort the little girl. A confusing look of "you'll be sorry" crept across her face, even while she continued her phone conversation. Her expression soon gave way to uncontrollable grinning as she finally hung up the phone. She motioned me into the other office as I finally coaxed the little girl to be seated.

"That was her mother on the phone," she finally said through open- throttled laughter.

"I sent for her to check out…because she has lice!"

Dear God,

"A time to embrace…and a time to refrain from embracing." Ecclesiastes. Old Testament. I got it.

Amen.

CHAPTER 8: WHERE'S RANDY?

൘

Blended families, put together through choice or circumstances, are always a challenge. A family tragedy that brought my nephew and niece to live with us changed our family dynamics tremendously and forever. Our youngest son, Randy, and his cousin, Eric, a few years older, became like brothers. Through junior high and high school, their growing-up adventures were fun to watch, scary to hear about, and never without an element of danger.

Always looking for relaxing, get-away places from the stress of ministry and education, we found a camp located on the edge of a bayou which led into a lake in one direction and wound several miles into the swamp in the other. The bayou was teeming with alligators and snakes, all visible with a spotlight at night, especially the alligators with their bright red eyes and armored bodies cruising like wagging torpedoes just beneath the muddy surface. The wooded swamp behind the camp was home to every Southern creature imaginable. The croaking concert at night was sometimes deafening! Of course, we had a canoe and paddles, outfitted for "frogging" or just playing in the murky bayou and back waters of this chunk of the great Atchafalaya swamp.

Being a father at any stage of your children's growing up years is not an easy task. The worries and what-ifs filling your mind during the day wake you up from a dead sleep at night. Their mental, physical, and emotional well-being is always foremost in your thinking and planning. Now, put all of that together with wanting to have fun raising them and wanting them to have fun growing up and the stage is set for this story.

It was a late summer, Saturday afternoon, and we were at the camp. The first part of the day had been spent cutting grass and goofing off…and boredom had set in. The boys decided it would be fun to paddle down the bayou into the swamp to see where it eventually went. Both were great swimmers and I wasn't too concerned. They donned life jackets, grabbed the paddles, and launched the canoe. I could hear them talking and laughing as they paddled in rhythm down the bayou, disappearing from sight in the hanging moss and twisted tree limbs.

A good cup of coffee and a few sermon notes later, I had dozed off and slept for the next few hours. I awoke with a start, noticing that the light outside had faded, and that I had not heard the boys' voices, since they left.

"Surely to God they're back," I thought…almost aloud.

Getting up from the sofa, and quickly exiting the back screen door, I noticed the boat was not back. Not prone to panic, I walked up to the roadway where the bayou meandered under the bridge. Staring down the bayou as far as I could see, I could detect no motion that looked like a little canoe, nor could I hear voices from the ever-darkening swamp. A glance at my watch told me it was nearly 5:00 PM and getting dark quickly. My heart began to race as I thought of every possible horrible thing that could have happened.

"What on earth are they doing," I muttered to no one.

As twilight set in, I heard the thudding of jogging-like steps coming toward me from the darkness. It was Eric.

"Is Randy back?" he asked as calmly as he could.

"No, he's not back! Where were you? Where is he? You left him in the swamp? How far back? Are you nuts?"

My questions were firing at him like a machine gun.

"Oh my god!" I yelled. "Now what are we going to do?" As we quickly ran down a list of possible actions, the top of the list was to call the sheriff's office. As we half-ran back to the camp, Eric, quite out of breath, began to detail their adventure.

"I saw this trail on the bank, and I wanted to see where it went. I told Randy that I might be back, but if not, then to start back for the camp. Pretty soon, I was too far away to go back to the boat because it was getting dark. So I cut across a cane field and came out on this road. I hitched a ride back to here, thinking Randy would be back."

Raw panic began to set in. Mosquitoes were viciously swarming, alligators were everywhere, and I knew Randy would hang around longer than anyone else, thinking Eric would return to the boat...a hunch that later proved correct. Just as I was about to call the sheriff's office, Eric had an idea.

"Why don't we get the neighbor to launch his big boat, and we can go looking for Randy. I think I know where I left him."

Strangely enough, that plan seemed plausible at the time. A few Bud Lights had mellowed the mood of the neighbor, but after hearing what had happened he became a willing, relatively sober participant in the search party.

About a mile into the alligator infested swamp, a very tired, mosquito-bitten, angry Randy paddled into view of the spotlight. Hiding the tears which welled up in my eyes, I swallowed hard and kept my mouth shut as he and Eric came to an understanding about their future adventures. They finally burst into laughter, and I knew everything was okay. All was well with the world...one more time.

Dear God,

Is cussing always a sin? Again, just asking.

Amen.

CHAPTER 9: JUST TRYING TO HELP

 C3

Our oldest son, now a dad himself, often asks me if I have any projects with which he can help. The very inquiry sends my mind sailing back to his growing up years and to his strong-willed, intense desire to help me any way he could do so. Our projects together were usually not much fun.

The early-American style rocking chair is still in good shape, after many hours and miles of rocking babies, neighbors' kids, and now grand kids It's one of those pieces of furniture that, had it been particularly valuable or well-built from the beginning, would be more appreciated for its workmanship rather than sentimentality. It's been moved a million times, as we relocated from place to place, and always the inevitable question, "Where are going to put the rocking chair?"

Ah yes, the rocking chair. We bought the thing from a discount furniture store in the town where we lived. Expecting Randy, our only biological offspring, found us searching for a rocking chair to match our motley collection of furniture. Our little girl, eighteen months old when we got her in foster care, and eight years old when the adoption was final, had no need of a rocker...except her "time out" rocker in the corner of her room.

Buying a rocking chair to rock the soon-to-be newborn just seemed like the thing to do. So we did. Maple colored, high-backed, and new. It took a position of prominence in the living room, and had to be tried out by each member of the family. Yep, it rocked just fine. Pictures of the baby being rocked abound. Christmas morning photos with paper and boxes strewn about find the rocking chair sitting proudly in the middle of the happy, annual chaos.

As though it were growing tired, the rocker began showing signs of joint failure. No amount of wood glue, nails, or clamps seemed to hold it together for more than a few sittings. One Saturday morning, after the chair's back spindles flayed apart just as an in-law sat down, I decided it was time to completely overhaul the rocker or get rid of it. I decided to give it an overhaul.

Jonathan, in his mid-teens, was anxious to help in the project of rocking chair restoration. I carefully dismantled the chair, taking care to place the varied length spindles in order on the carport floor. Next, I had to trim the right length off each spindle, taking care to keep the ratios correct. Next, I had to drill out the holes on the seat of the chair so that the altered spindles would fit snugly. My son watched intently, handing me things as I worked.

"A quiet bonding moment; we haven't argued at all. This is good," I thought, very pleased with myself.

"You can't even tell we fixed it," I bragged as I placed the last spindle in place.

"Once I anchor them with these little wire brads, the glue will dry, and they'll hold for a long time."

Jonathan didn't say anything. I just knew he was accepting my wisdom and marveling at my carpentry skills, probably somewhat jealous. Yeah, that's what I was thinking. The phone rang and I had to go inside. I told him to just watch the rocker, don't let anyone sit in it, and I'd be right back.

"Okay, dad, I'll do that."

The phone call lasted about thirty minutes. That's how long it takes to be jarred from feeling like you've accomplished something to complete frustration. While I was on the phone, the overwhelming need to build a better mousetrap must have kicked in.

35

I came back out to our project to find a four-inch screw sticking out of the seat of the rocker, aimed at one of the spindles, now cracked.

"What did you do?" was about all I could say.

"I didn't think your little nails would hold so I decided to put screws instead," he responded without looking up, still twisting on the stripped-out head of the three-inch screw.

I'm looking at the rocker as I write. Years have gone by and the putty-filled hole still grins back at me. There were many life lessons I had to learn, but this one was tough.

"He was just trying to help," was his mom's defense for him.

I just wanted a complete, brag-worthy project, done with relative ease. What I got was a life lesson about allowing help. Sometimes you get what you need and long for. Sometimes you get a four-inch screw. The intentions, not necessarily the results, must count for something!

Dear God,

Do you think being such a perfectionist that no one wants to help me is a sin or a strategy?

Amen.

CHAPTER 10: LET'S GO RAFTING!

℃ℨ

The rafting trip from hell. That's what it was.

Beautiful sunshiny day, rapids running like rapids do, in the company of three delightful young people. What could be better?

Although I know I looked totally moronic in the little yellow helmet, I grinned and looked like I was having fun…even though I was shivering in fear that the raft would flip. Pigeon Forge, Tennessee. Dolly Parton. Tennessee. Nothing could be better. Standing in line for what seemed like an hour, we finally loaded up on the old bus, all helmeted and life-jacketed up, ready for a cool, rafting adventure. That was me, alright…the very essence of cool.

The preload instructions from the "guide" had sounded easy enough.

"Paddle when I say paddle. Stop when I say stop."

I had this. Oh, did I mention that a freckle-faced, tousled hair rookie guide, completing his training, was to serve as our "trip guide" while his supervisor was evaluating him? I've decided that the very last thing you want to hear from your rookie guide, as you slam into a boulder in the middle of the river, is "My bad."

Those are the only words that registered as my air borne rear-end came up from the seat and sailed over the side of the raft.

"This isn't happening to me because I don't really want to be here without a raft," I thought as I struggled hard to maintain dignity while reaching futilely for my now-daughter-in-law's extended paddle.

My son and our other friend could have possibly been of some help had they been able to control their laughter. The rushing, splashing river was merciless. I shot head first through a number four rapid, without the benefit of the raft, and went spiraling toward the river-bottom at a speed I didn't know my body was capable of performing.

"This really sucks. What if I drown? What if no one finds me?"

My answers all came, albeit briefly, when I got vomited up from the depths by the same force that sucked me under, just to repeat the fun plunge again. Oh my God! I had been tossed out of a raft into number four rapids, sloshed and bumped down the river a hundred yards, while choking down at least ten gallons of ice-cold river water!

I'll never forget my flailing, humiliating sensations of helplessness as the break-neck river dunked me at will down that Tennessee mountain! I might also add that having grinning teenagers, fighting back the urge to double over laughing, hoist me back out of the river into the international orange, bouncing rubber raft was not the coolest feeling in the world.

I don't think I spoke to any of them until the next day. My ego was basically ruined. My behind ached, and I never wanted to taste river water again. I was thrown out of my safety zone…and survived.

Dear God,

Why can't I bring myself to use "too old" as an excuse?

Amen.

CHAPTER 11: YOU HAVE HIS CUP

ℭℬ

The art of making ministerial home visits can be a little precarious at times. Dressing the right way, saying the right things, and reacting the right way are just a few of the talents required to make a successful home visit. I found out early on that being a coffee drinker, especially in the South, was a huge plus in building rapport with the community.

I had heard of a family in need in the community, and I decided to investigate and offer my assistance. I put on my navy blue pastor suit, brushed my teeth and hair, and headed off, yet again, to change the world. The family lived in a cramped mobile home, situated on a gravel road between two bayous. Some of the children were chasing each other around the parked car with flat tires sitting in the driveway while others were sitting on the edge of the little front-door porch, legs dangling and swinging from the edge.

All actions stopped when I pulled up. The kids paused in their activities and began whispering to each other. Their mother came to the door and nodded. Quickly, I introduced myself as the new minister in the community and added that I just wanted to stop by to say hello.

"Oh, you the new priest," she replied, motioning for me to come on in.

I ascended the four steps onto the porch, followed by a line of children, each one curiously looking me over. I tried to explain that I wasn't the new priest, but I was the new pastor of the little church up the road.

"Same thing," she said and asked me if I'd like to sit down.

From the back of the trailer, the wiry, thin, shirtless father came into the living room, carrying their snarling, lunging little black and white spotted Chihuahua.

"He tries to act bad, but he won't hurt you," he assured me.

"Do you drink coffee?" the lady of the house asked.

"I got a sample in the mail, and I want to try it out" she further explained.

"That sounds great," I spoke up cheerily, "I love instant coffee."

Engaged in conversation with the kids and the father, I was oblivious to the coffee preparations underway. She came over and handed me a rough-edged plastic cup with some of the foulest tasting coffee I had ever attempted to drink.

"I can't read too good, but it had a one and a three on the side of the jar. So I put one cup of water and three spoons of coffee. Oh yeah, I put three spoons of sugar in it too."

Not a connoisseur of sweet coffee, I knew that was going to be a problem. When I read the directions, the "one and the three" referred to 1/3 of a tablespoon of coffee per cup of hot water. This would be a problem, but I had to attempt to drink it….maybe in little sips.

The Chihuahua, aptly named "T-T," kept up his snarling and snipping, but seemed to get louder and more frantic as I sipped my coffee. Soon, he and I established a rhythm … I'd sip, and he'd yelp louder. Sip….yelp. I looked at the mother…then at the dad…then at all the kids gathered around…and then at the dog.

"Watch," I said. "Each time I sip, he goes nuts," thinking I had magical powers over him.

"You want to know why?" the oldest son offered.

"Sure. Why?"

"Cause you're drinking out of his cup."

Well, that explained the rough edges. Closer examination revealed his bite marks on the handle. I was drinking from his play toy. The mother tried to make it a little better, though.

She admonished the dog with, "T-T, stop barking. You can have your cup back when he finishes his coffee."

I seriously had to go at that point. A quick glance at my wrist watch suddenly reminded me of a previous engagement. A lie, but necessary. I got about half a mile away, jerked open the car door and threw up.

Dear God,

When will I be able to throw up other people's bitter stuff without feeling guilty?

Amen.

CHAPTER 12: MORE CRABS? NO, THANKS.

℘

You just can't live in the Deep South and not be a lover of great seafood. Crawfish, oysters, crabs, fried catfish. Oh, wow. Just thinking about such great things makes me hungry.

I vividly remember the last time I ate big, freshwater, blue-clawed crabs, caught fresh that very day! We got the invitation late in the day and the crabs had already been put on to boil.

"Y'all come over right now. They're almost ready."

It didn't take but a minute to scramble the kids into the car and head over to our friend's house for the crab boil.

You see, crawfish boils and crab boils in south Louisiana aren't just crab or crawfish boils. Into the boiling, heavily seasoned tub of water goes whole onions, corn on the cob, links of sausage, and whatever else is available! The flavors all blended together are delicious! A long, wooden plank table with a hole in the middle to shove leftovers into facilitates the asynchronous crunching of crab shells, wrenching and sucking bits of meat from the crab's insides, and makes for incredible fun and relaxation with the families.

We arrived just as the first basket of boiled crabs was dumped out onto the table. Steam rose from the pile of crabs as we all grabbed a chair, pulled up to the table and started pounding. Good stuff. Good conversation, too.

"Did y'all hear about that guy that drowned last week?" our hostess asked.

"Yeah," I said, "that was a shame."

The list of everyone he was related to followed, although no one I knew was on the list. A detailed account of the boating accident was delivered by one of the kids; followed by a round of silence, save for the crunching of crab claws and the sucking down of the tidbits of meat.

The hot, spicy Cajun seasoning was perfect.

"How do you know how to season these things so well?" I inquired, complimenting our host.

"This is great!"

He went down his seasoning list for me, including everything from cayenne pepper to liquid crab boil...

"But you know what really makes them good?" he asked.

"They have to be fat. The fat holds the seasoning," he added, "these are fat."

I thoughtfully nodded my head, glanced at my wife who was coaxing a bit of meat from a cracked claw, and dug into another crab.

"Yeah," our hostess continued, "they never found that poor guy. They dragged for days, but nothing turned up."

"A shame," I said almost mechanically as I chased a mouthful of crab with a swig of Diet Coke.

"All I know," she continued, "...these crabs sure are fat."

I stopped mid-swig, processing what I just heard. Oh my gosh. My wife was about to faint. I was about to faint. There, on that beautiful Saturday afternoon, my crab-eating days ended. Nope, no more crabs for me.

Dear God,

Does saying grace before a meal take care of things like this? Just asking.

Amen.

CHAPTER 13: YOU DROWNED MY DADDY!

⍩

The little church was full that Sunday night, each pew packed with local folks, waiting to witness the baptism of Mr. Morvant.

As I stood waist-deep in the baptistery, my white robe soaked to my chest, I thought back to the events that had brought us to this solemn moment in the 82-year-old life of Mr. Morvant.

Feeling quite pastoral, I thought it a great idea to recount those events, in my best up-and-down ministerial voice, and then bring it all to a crescendo with Mr. Morvant taking the plunge into the baptismal waters. So I began Mr. Morvant's tale....

"It was just a regular Sunday morning," I began, "while teaching the young people's Bible class, I heard a knock on the front door of the church..."

"Good morning! Can I help you?"

Peering back at me was a thin, elderly gentleman in a time-stamped suit, and his middle- aged son, wearing a well-worn, brown derby hat.

"He wants to tell you something," his son, removing his hat in reverence for the moment, leaned over and whispered to me.

"I want to come to this church," the older gentleman began in very broken Cajun French and English.

"Come on in!"

A little astonished, I eagerly welcomed both men into the church sanctuary. Nervously, quietly chatting in French, the two sat down on the last pew.

The cluster of teenagers who were in my Bible class that morning hung curiously out the classroom door, puzzled as they gazed down the church aisle to where the two gentlemen sat.

"What did they want?" they inquired, and not too quietly.

"He wants to come to church here," I told them, as they collectively mouthed, "Oh."

Feeding on the "*awhs*" and "*amens*" of the crowd gathered for the baptism, I summoned the rest of my spiritual fuel and burned on. I continued to tell Mr. Morvant's story…

"After a few weeks of coming to church regularly and faithfully," I continued, "Mr. Morvant decided he wanted to be baptized …and here we are."

The church erupted in applause and spontaneous singing of "*God is so Good.*" Tears and chills…and Mr. Morvant would soon be baptized.

My attention to Mr. Morvant's nervous arrival at the top of the baptistery stairs was interrupted by the arrival of his daughter in the rear of the sanctuary, being greeted with hugs and kisses by community friends gathered for the event. Pointing and gesturing toward the baptistery and the impending event, she finally took her seat in the only available space on the back row of pews. I noticed her distraught-appearing countenance, but my ministerial mind, at a full throttle, decided she was overcome with spiritual exhilaration. Yeah. That was it. Spiritual exhilaration.

My interest again was focused on Mr. Morvant, standing quietly, pale and thin, clad in his baptismal robe. I reached up from the baptistery to take his hand, to steady him down into the water.

"Mr. Morvant," I whispered. No response.

"Mr. Morvant!" I whispered a little louder. Slowly, his hand extended toward mine, and he shakily made his way down the three grated steps into the water.

Now the proper technique for baptizing an adult, according to practitioners of the craft, is to hold the back of the candidate with one hand and, using a white handkerchief, cover the nose and mouth with the other. Then, as the candidate bends at the knees and leans backward, he is quickly lowered into the water and lifted right back up. Mr. Morvant and I had a dry-run at it, so I knew it would go well.

"Going well" was not to be. Not this time. As I placed my right hand on his back and gently covered his face with my handkerchief and left hand, I began the baptismal ritual. "In the name of the Father, Son, and Holy Ghost," I prayed and lowered him into the water. That's when it all went haywire. Instead of bending at the knees, Mr. Morvant's body went completely rigid, eyes tightly shut, feet straight out, in full float in front of me. He held my handkerchief hand in a death grip that was not to be broken. "Mr. Morvant? Mr. Morvant? Mr. Morvant?" Help me Lord. Now what?

My lightening-fast, non-spiritual mind kicked in. I couldn't think of anything to do except to float him over to the side and try to angle his rigid legs downward toward one of the steps. I figured then I could leverage him into an upright position, and that he'd snap back to life! My efforts in the baptistery had me completely oblivious to the mood change of the crowd. As I floated Mr. Morvant toward the steps, the crowd had risen to its feet and bum-rushed the podium, trying to get a better view. Just as his feet touched the steps, at my downward shove of his legs, his daughter shrieked at the top of her lungs, "You drowned my daddy!"

47

The gasp that filled the sanctuary gave me the immediate impression that the crowd also believed her conclusion. I'm sure the moan of the group could have been heard for miles!

"Mr. Morvant!" I shouted.

Mr. Morvant, still clutching my handkerchief hand, opened one eye and coarsely whispered, "Is it over?"

I leaned over to his good ear and sighed, "Yes…it's over."

In one swift, fluid gesture, he made the sign of the cross, and yelled, "Thank God!" and climbed right out of the tank.

The crowd, of course, broke into one more round of *"God is so Good."*

Dear God,

When you laugh, does it sound like the chorus, *"God is so Good?"* Just wondering.

Amen.

Chapter 14: The Teacher's Teacher

ℭℨ

I started college in the Fall of 1969 with no clue of what my life journey was to be.

Vietnam was raging; the draft was in full swing; and a college deferment was a more sought-after piece of paper than a diploma.

By the time I won the draft lottery (the only thing I've won in my life), President Nixon had facilitated the U.S. exit from the war, and the deferment pressure had subsided a bit, I did manage to squeeze four years of college into six and a half years, with more drops and adds, major changes, and redirects than anyone in the world.

Marriage, finishing school, entering the ministry, and starting a little church all happened almost simultaneously. When my wife and I moved to the community where the little church started, she became a second grade teacher in the school there. Substitute teaching at the school helped me find the passion and focus that would define my life. I wrapped up my undergraduate work with a double major in social studies and speech education! I couldn't wait to get started making a difference!

After a couple of interviews, I was offered my first teaching position at Morgan City High School, in the days of the oil boom in South Louisiana. I remember accepting the position, offered just as I completed student teaching, with a sense of pride and importance like I'd never known. I was, at last, a teacher. It was like Christmas.

The slate of classes I was assigned included American History, Civics, Economics, and Study Hall. I would be replacing a veteran teacher retiring at mid-term. Another teacher, retiring after a long tenure of service, gave me her parting advice as she prepared to exit the profession.

"Mr. Douglas," she said in a low, hushed tone. "I have two pieces of unasked-for advice. First, speak softly…don't yell…so they'll have to listen to hear you. Secondly, you'll have to find them before you can lead them."

"I've got this," I stupidly thought to myself, graciously thanking her for her words of wisdom. Holding tightly the key to the door to my classroom, I quietly entered what was to become my very own second floor chamber of horrors. That January, Friday afternoon, the room was dark, smelled like stale cigarette smoke, and the desks, books, and the teacher's desk were in utter disarray.

I remember thinking, "The maintenance crew just hasn't cleaned yet."

The following Monday was to be the beginning of my real education about education. Just calling roll seemed like the challenge of a lifetime. I quickly discovered that much of what I had learned in college about teaching could be scrapped. I also learned that mispronouncing names of high school students is akin to insulting someone's mother.

First hour students shoved through the door, eying me up suspiciously as I waited.

"Who the hell is this?" one asked aloud, to no one in particular.

"Must be a substitute," a nameless voice answered.

"Nope, he's our new teacher," someone chimed in.

"Is he straight? Yep, he's got a wedding ring. Straight."

"Where's he from?"

"He drives a Mazda. I saw him the parking lot."

This whole conversation reset and replayed at every class exchange that first day.

For this I sweated the draft, too many college credits, and, only the Lord knows how much tuition?

As I glanced at the first hour class, I realized that a couple of the kids were from the youth group at the church where I was pastor. The most interesting thing about them was that they completely ignored me, preferring instead, to remain anonymous in that setting. I didn't blame them. I would have preferred anonymity, too.

As the day wore on, I interrupted a suspicious cigarette rolling pursuit, encouraged a student to stop soliciting names from the class for her unborn child, and discreetly quashed a front-row gentleman's under the desk-top activities.

Oh, yes. Education. Got to love it.

Dear God,

When I'm busy making my life plans, could you please pay closer attention?

Amen.

CHAPTER 15: SUNDAY LUNCH

❧

Remarkably, few experiences in the Deep South come close to the tradition of Sunday Lunch, an after-church affair that creates a family and friend bonding time like no other. The menu almost universally includes something deep-fried, mashed potatoes and gravy, and homemade bread rolls…generally hosted at someone's grandmother's home. Lunch invitations, spontaneous and inclusive, are usually extended on the fly, with each guest expected to bring something. The pastor's family, though, is never expected to bring anything but hearty appetites…and that's exactly what we did!

It was an October Sunday, cool, breezy, and perfect for a great after-church, deep-fried lunch. The invitation from one of the church families came just as church service wrapped up that morning.

"Y'all got plans for lunch?" Whitney asked.

"Not yet," I shot back.

"You do now. We'll see y'all at the house."

Whitney and Waverly were two of the most animated people I'd ever met. Never having to worry what they were thinking, they were generous to a fault, funny beyond belief, and as blunt as could be. Waverly, diabetic and often sick, didn't just enter a room…she exploded into it with whatever thought was on her mind. Whitney, an entrepreneur and caretaker for his wife, struggled with his own health issues, and worked hard to make ends meet. Both long gone now, I still laugh aloud at some of the adventures we experienced, having never met anyone like them since.

Whitney had fenced in part of their backyard, penning up ducks, a turkey or two, and a few chickens.

Never at a loss for a dog, the fence kept the foul safe from roving strays, dropped off along the levee highway which ran in front of their converted house-boat home.

Each of their animals, chickens included, all had names and personalities. Helen was a black and white spotted hen, a good laying hen. Esmerelda, a Rhode Island Red, was a huge, cantankerous hen, and the defender of the backyard crew. The ducks, Donald and Lulu, were just nasty, and content to parade around in the mud and muck. Esmerelda, the sentinel, was always the first to sprint flapping and squawking, neck extended, across the backyard to the fence to check us out or snatch up breadcrumbs whenever we visited. Her antics were usually a topic conversation and laughter.

"Church was boring this morning," Waverly called out from the living room as we walked in.

"It wasn't your fault, I just wasn't in the mood."

"Okay, as long as it wasn't my fault," I joked back. Whitney, the cook of the family was busy at the stove, painting butter onto the bread rolls and preparing the rest of the meal.

"Lunch smells delicious!" My mouth watered as we chatted and waited for lunch. Finally, at Whitney's invitation, we shuffled into the kitchen and settled into assigned spots at the kitchen table.

The golden brown, homemade rolls, glistening from their melted butter bath, filled the air with aromas of childhood, the school cafeteria, and good times. The mashed potatoes, uniquely seasoned with a blend of garlic, chives, and who-knows-what, were a steaming, welcomed addition to the table as we watched. At last, the final addition…battered and deep fried chicken, smoking hot and filling the air with delicious anticipation!

"Y'all dig in!" Whitney commanded, waiting for our oohs and ahhs as we took our first bites. "I've got your favorite dessert in the fridge…banana pudding!" Oh my gosh.

Never one to be asked twice to dig in, I loaded my plate and started feasting. I love dark meat, and didn't hesitate to spear both legs and a thigh. Gravy on the potatoes, extra butter on the rolls, and I was ready to eat. The only conversation that took place from then on was in short sentences, punctuated by a swallow and another bite.

The deep-fried thigh was crunchy and delicious! The first leg, coated with a heavy crispy fried batter, was incredible. The second leg, though, had a little different story. When I picked it up to take a bite, it bent, broken, toward my plate. "That's weird, Whitney. What's up with this leg?" I should have kept my mouth shut.

"Some damned dog," he started. "Should've shot him. You remember Esmerelda…the big red hen…well that dog got in the backyard and broke her leg and killed her. I could either cry or fry. So, how dies she taste?"

Dear God,

So the Whitney approach of "you can either cry or fry" is a life lesson?

Amen.

CHAPTER 16: A PEN, PLEASE.

⁂

I was only a few years into my high school teaching career and was flying high! Not yet thirty and I was *the* popular teacher that students wanted to schedule, *the* witty instructor who delivered on quality education! Yep, that was me. I had the ego thing under control, too.

I know why God created adolescence as the final phase of human development before adulthood…it's so that when teenagers become so obnoxious that you can no longer stand being around them, you're actually *relieved* when then leave home…or graduate! High school teachers go through the same love-hate relationships with teenagers. Some days you love being around them…other days, you pray they're absent.

This gray, drizzly, dismal day was one of those.

"Wouldn't it be wonderful if it were junior-senior skip out day…" I daydreamed, winding my way around the lake to the school.

Pulling into the parking lot brought me back to reality. All of their cars were in their assigned spaces. Shucks. Grabbing my briefcase and the freshly-graded stack of world history tests which, based on their grades, I had apparently written in Greek, I trudged up the ramp to the front doors, and up to my second story classroom.

Realizing my mood needed to change or the day was likely going to be incredibly long and laborious, I repeated the scripture, almost aloud, "This is the day the Lord has made; I will rejoice and be glad in it."

As I took a deep, refreshing breath, the bell rang.

"High expectations. That's it. I have to have high expectations."

My mental mantra found its way to my voice. First period class filed in, yawning and stretching, and I began the roll call in the most lack-luster voice I could find.

"Answer the roll, please," I droned.

"Class, I have high expectations of you. Your grades on the test yesterday did not meet my expectations. We are going to go over the material again, and you'll have an opportunity to demonstrate your knowledge again tomorrow."

Wow. I sounded so *the* teacher. However, my struggle to "rejoice in the day" didn't last long. My rant about their lousy test grades was much more fulfilling.

We launched into a review of the lecture notes, a class activity not exactly welcomed with smiles and glee. It took one class exchange for the word to spread that Douglas was ticked off and was going to re-test tomorrow. Second period was my planning period, so I had plenty of time to hone my griping spiel by the time third period rolled around.

The third period class was an amusing bunch…and my favorite class. I'm not sure how they all got grouped together, but there they were. They laughed the loudest at my lame jokes, poked fun at each other without mercy, and viewed me as their teacher-project whose reputation for being cool had to be coached and preserved. I trusted them for a moment as I hustled down the hall to the water fountain.

It only took a minute or two to get a quick drink of water, and when I got back to the class they were seated, quiet, and had their notebooks open, ready to work. I knew then, without a doubt, that my "high expectations" speech the first hour had spread, and that they did not want to disappoint me. In fact, before I could begin, one of the guys volunteered," Mr. D, we didn't do so hot on the test yesterday…could we review and re-test tomorrow?"

"You see, that's why I love this class," I told them. "You take responsibility for your learning and you're actually pleasant to teach. Thank you!"

The class spokesman raised his hand.

"Do you have a pen I could borrow?" he asked in humble earnestness.

"Sure!" I walked over to my desk and noticed my "Go Army" pencil cup was not in its usual place.

Puzzled, I pulled open the squeaky desk drawer and found the pencil cup…*and* a very real-looking plastic replica of male genitalia with a note attached. The note read "DON'T BE ONE OF THESE" and was simply signed "Your Loving Students."

Well, having taught teenagers awhile, and with no way of proving who the culprit was, I knew the importance of thinking on my feet…and keeping a sense of perspective and humor. I pretended I had not seen the "gift" and reached for an ink pen from the pencil cup. I handed the pen to the precocious gent who had asked for it, and I strolled back to my speaker's stand. "I forgot to call the roll,"" I said, as they looked at each other, shrugging and puzzled.

"David?"

"Here."

"Brian?"

"Here."

"Richard? "Richard?" No answer.

Without missing a beat, I walked over to the desk drawer, slid it open, and said "Oh, there you are!" The class erupted in relieved laughter. I had gotten the message. Lesson learned.

Dear God,

When dealing with teenagers, sometimes laughing is better, right?

Amen

CHAPTER 17: TAKE ON A TUGBOAT

ᘓ

Phineas was a strange little dog. He was the offspring of a dainty poodle mother and a hearty, field-tested beagle father; a tireless hunter with a splash of class! The funny thing about this dog… he never quite understood his limitations. He seemed never to grasp the notion that dogs don't climb trees— even if the squirrel goes up one. He never really comprehended that he wasn't a German Shepherd or a Doberman and boldly challenged any creature that wandered into his territory.

Chasing quacking, flapping ducks off the bank, and diving in after them into the muddy south Louisiana bayou, was a much-practiced routine for Phineas. In fact, he spent much of his day barking, chasing, swimming and barking some more. Anything that moved—whether winged or four-footed—was fair game for his frantic pursuits.

One late Saturday afternoon, the challenge of a beagle-poo's lifetime came. Rounding the curve of the bayou, slowly chugging down the murky waterway, huffing billows of diesel smoke into the evening air was a tugboat, shoving a barge load of oyster shells to its destination. Yep, a tugboat.

As though momentarily suspended in dog-mind contemplation, Phineas eyed up his next target. His wagging tail, which had been still while he "thought", began to twitch with a fervor like never before. He didn't know he *couldn't*. Into the water he splashed, swimming frenetically and yelping like his tail was on fire! Around the bend the tugboat and barge chugged, Phineas in pursuit. A couple of hours later, a wet and thoroughly exhausted little mutt returned home. He didn't catch the tug, but he danged sure tried.

As I swayed forwards and backwards in the old cypress swing suspended from the oak tree beside the bayou, I had to admit…the little mutt amazed me! I actually got his message!

When you've climbed all your trees and the ducks have all flown, take on a tugboat! Refuse to accept your limits and embrace your potential. Yes! This was the "Zen" moment I was looking for! There were Cathedrals to pastor, ignorance to stamp out, third world countries to feed, and incurable diseases to cure! My Phineas.

Through the years of meeting people, observing and being observed, leading and being led, I've learned much about people but so much more about myself.

Shortcuts usually take longer; the easy way out rarely is; "let me pray about it" are code words for *heck no*; what goes around doesn't always come around; and absolutely nothing in life is free.

I've also learned that the one who never embraces a challenge, never really knows the outer limits of his potential. If just being content is the goal, then we'll never explore the painted horizons of an evening sunset in the hills of new territory or on the waves of uncharted seas—or the freshness of a new morning's sunrise, pregnant with possibilities.

In ministry and in teaching, the voice of new adventure has been barking all along. It is the *Phineas* in me that needs to chase a few ducks and climb a few trees! It is the God-given rite of passage from one definition of who I am to another. In fact, maybe it is *the* definition of who I am; a divine DNA that longs for the freedom to be everything I was designed to be! Who says we can't take on a new challenge? Who says we can't press past the boundaries of someone else's limitations? Who says we can't take on a tugboat?

So…when my ducks have all flown and all of my trees have been climbed, it'll be time for a new challenge. I'll take on a tugboat. I may not catch it, and I may not know what to do with it if I did, but look out tug-boat, here I come! When the chase is over, I'll have just one more prayer….

Dear God,

How did I do?

Amen.

About the Author

Wendell C. Douglas is a native of Lafourche Parish, Louisiana. He holds undergraduate and graduate degrees in education from Nicholls State University in Thibodaux, Louisiana. With a doctorate in Christian Counseling, he has also been an ordained minister and life coach for over twenty-five years.

A professional educator and spiritual advisor, having served as a pastor, teacher, school administrator, university instructor, and educational consultant, Dr. Wendell Douglas has a rich background in educational leadership, teaching, K-12 public school administration, faculty development, the evaluation of effective teaching and learning, and life coaching.

As a personal and professional development coach and consultant, Dr. Douglas provides in-service training and consultation to parents, church groups, individuals, organizations, and professional educators in the areas of family dynamics, group facilitation skills, peer coaching, learning preferences, study skills, effective communication strategies, management skills, conferencing skills, and interpersonal relationship development.

Visit online at http://douglasconsults.com

LaVergne, TN USA
01 December 2009
165628LV00002B/205/P